D0604529

CULTURES CONNECT US!

FOLKTALES

BY CYRIL BASSINGTON

Gareth Stevens
PUBLISHING

Please visit our website, www.garethstevens.com. For a free color catalog of all our high-quality books, call toll free 1-800-542-2595 or fax 1-877-542-2596.

Cataloging-in-Publication Data

Names: Bassington, Cyril.
Title: Folktales / Cyril Bassington.
Description: New York : Gareth Stevens Publishing, 2020. | Series: Cultures connect us! | Includes glossary and index.
Identifiers: ISBN 9781538238387 (pbk.) | ISBN 9781538238400 (library bound) | ISBN 9781538238394 (6 pack)
Subjects: LCSH: Folklore–Juvenile literature.
Classification: LCC GR74.B374 2020 | DDC 398.2–dc23

Published in 2020 by
Gareth Stevens Publishing
111 East 14th Street, Suite 349
New York, NY 10003

Copyright © 2020 Gareth Stevens Publishing

Designer: Reann Nye
Editor: Therese Shea

Photo credits: series art (background) Lukasz Szwaj/Shutterstock.com; cover Edgar Lee Espe/Shutterstock.com; p. 5 Kristina Sophie/Shutterstock.com; p. 7 imtmphoto/ Shutterstock.com; p. 9 duncan1890/DigitalVision Vectors/Getty Images; p. 11 Jean Ignace Isidore Gérard Grandville/https://commons.wikimedia.org/wiki/ File:Grandville_tortoise.jpg; p. 13 ZU_09/DigitalVision Vectors/Getty Images; p. 15 Arthur Rackham/https://commons.wikimedia.org/wiki/File:Arthur_Rackham_ Little_Red_Riding_Hood%2B.jpg; p. 17 CSA Images/Vetta/Getty Images; p. 19 Yoshitoshi/https://commons.wikimedia.org/wiki/File:Yoshitoshi_-_100_Aspects_of_ the_Moon_-_91.jpg; p. 21 Sergey Novikov/Shutterstock.com.

All rights reserved. No part of this book may be reproduced in any form without permission in writing from the publisher, except by a reviewer.

Printed in the United States of America

CPSIA compliance information: Batch #CS19GS: For further information contact Gareth Stevens, New York, New York at 1-800-542-2595.

CONTENTS

Boldface words appear in the glossary.

Pieces of Culture

Culture is the ways of life of a group of people. It includes the music they listen to, the clothes they wear, the languages they speak, the foods they eat, and much, much more! It also includes the stories they tell.

Passing Down Stories

All cultures around the world have told stories since before history was recorded. The stories weren't written down at first. They were spoken. Some of these stories were folktales. Folktales were **entertaining**, but they often also taught the values of a people.

Fables

Sometimes **characters** in folktales are animals that act like people! Fables are folktales that use animals to teach lessons. The most famous are the fables of Aesop (EE-sahp). It's said this Greek man first told these tales more than 2,000 years ago.

Aesop

9

Aesop's fable "The Tortoise and the Hare" is about a proud hare who thinks he can beat a tortoise in a race. The hare even takes a nap during the race! The tortoise wins. The lesson is: You can **succeed** through hard work.

11

Fairy Tales

Because folktales were spoken at first, there can be many **versions**. Different storytellers told different details. "Cinderella" is a kind of folktale called a fairy tale. There are many versions of this story. All teach that kindness and love are **rewarded**.

German brothers Jacob and Wilhelm Grimm began writing down folktales in Europe in the early 1800s. Today, we know these as *Grimm's Fairy Tales.* "Snow White," "Rapunzel," and "Little Red Riding Hood" are some of the famous tales they recorded.

15

Tall Tales

Tall tales are folktales with **details** that are greatly **exaggerated**. They sometimes explain why things happened. In America, there are tall tales about a giant **lumberjack** named Paul Bunyan. He's said to have made the Grand Canyon by dragging his ax on the ground!

17

Trickster Tales

Trickster folktales **feature** characters that try to trick others. African tales feature the spider Anansi. The Japanese trickster fox, Kitsune, sometimes takes human shape. Native American tales feature Coyote or Hare. American slaves told folktales about Brer Rabbit based on Hare.

Kitsune

19

Sharing Stories, Sharing Cultures

You probably know many of the folktales in this book. As people of different cultures came together as communities, they shared tales with each other. What other folktales do you know? What lessons or values do they teach you?

GLOSSARY

character: a person or creature who appears in a story

detail: a small part of something

entertaining: enjoyable

exaggerate: to think of or describe something as larger or greater than it really is

feature: to have or include as an important part

lumberjack: a person whose job is to cut down trees for wood

reward: to give someone something for good that has been done

succeed: to achieve a wanted result

version: a form of something that is different from others

FOR MORE INFORMATION

BOOKS

Arrington, H. J. *Anansi's Narrow Waist: A Tale from Ghana*. Gretna, LA: Pelican Publishing Company, 2016.

Grimm, Jacob, and Wilhelm Grimm. *Grimms' Fairy Tales*. New York, NY: Scholastic Inc., 2016.

Randolph, Joanne, ed. *Early American Legends and Folktales*. New York, NY: Cavendish Square Publishing, 2018.

WEBSITES

American Folktales and Stories
www.americanfolklore.net/sindex.html
Find links to many folktales here.

Discovering Fairy Tales
teacher.scholastic.com/writewit/mff/fairytales_discovering.htm
Read more about how magical folktales are connected.

Publisher's note to educators and parents: Our editors have carefully reviewed these websites to ensure that they are suitable for students. Many websites change frequently, however, and we cannot guarantee that a site's future contents will continue to meet our high standards of quality and educational value. Be advised that students should be closely supervised whenever they access the internet.

INDEX